Common Core Standards
Practice and Review

PEARSON

Boston, Massachusetts   Chandler, Arizona   Glenview, Illinois   Upper Saddle River, New Jersey

Table of Contents

Common Core Standards Practice

Week 1

Selected Response

1. Which of the following statements is true?

   A A line is part of a segment.
   B A line is part of a ray.
   C A plane contains a finite number of lines.
   D A line extends in two opposite directions without end.

Constructed Response

2. Points M, K, L, and J lie on a line.
   a. Label points on the line so that J is between M and L, $ML = 11$, $KL = 14$, and $KJ = 9$.

   ⟵─────────────────────⟶

   b. What is MJ?

Extended Response

3. $\angle ABC$ and $\angle CBD$ form a linear pair. $m\angle ABC = 3x + 10$ and $m\angle CBD = 22x + 45$.

   a. Find x.

   b. Find $m\angle ABC$ and $m\angle CBD$.

   c. Show how you can check your answer.

Common Core Standards Practice

Week 2

Selected Response

1. What is the midpoint of the line segment connecting $(-2, 7)$ and $(4, 15)$?

   A $(3, 11)$
   B $(1, 11)$
   C $(1, 22)$
   D $(1, 8)$

Constructed Response

2. Construct $\overline{AB}$ so that $FG + JK = AB$.

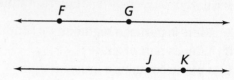

Extended Response

3. **a.** Consider the points $A(2, 8)$, $B(5, 4)$, $C(-1, 4)$, $D(-4, 0)$. Find AB, AC, AD, BC, BD, and CD.

   b. Write the names of the segments in the correct cell of the table.

Length of Segment = 5	Length of Segment ≠ 5

Common Core Standards Practice   Week 3

Selected Response

1. Is the following statement true? If it is false, choose a correct counterexample.

    If a number is prime, then it is odd.

    A True
    B False; 4 is even.
    C False; 15 is odd.
    D False; 2 is even.

2. What are the next two terms in the sequence?

    a, d, g, j, m,...

    A p, s
    B n, o
    C n, q
    D m, p

Constructed Response

3. Use the Law of Detachment to draw a conclusion. If it is not possible, then state why.

    If you get in your car, then you will drive to the store.

    You are seen shopping at the store.

Extended Response

4. The points J, K, and L are arranged on the line as shown below.   Prove that $x=4.5$. Fill in the blanks using the following reasons:
Transitive Property of Equality, Given, Substitution, Division Property of Equality.

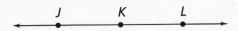

Statements	Reasons
1) $JK = KL$	1) Given
2) $JK = 3x + 9$	2) Given
3) $KL = 3x + 9$	3) _____
4) $JL = JK + KL$	4) Segment Addition Postulate
5) $JL = 3x + 9 + 3x + 9$	5) _____
6) $JL = 6x + 18$	6) Combining Like Terms
7) $JL = 45$	7) _____
8) $6x + 18 = 45$	8) Transitive Property of Equality
9) $6x = 27$	9) Subtraction Property of Equality
10) $x = 4.5$	10) _____

Common Core Standards Practice

Week 4

Selected Response

1. If $m\angle 3 = 131$, what is $m\angle 6$?

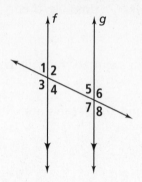

A 41
B 49
C 131
D 229

Constructed Response

2. $\angle A$ and $\angle B$ are alternate interior angles formed by two parallel lines and a transversal. $m\angle A = 4x - 7$ and $m\angle B = 89$. Find x.

Extended Response

3. Prove that $r \parallel s$ if $\angle 1$ and $\angle 7$ are supplementary by writing the correct reason in the appropriate place.

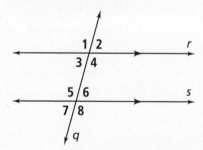

Fill in the blanks using the following reasons:
- Substitution Property
- Converse of the Same-Side Interior Angles Postulate
- Vertical Angles Theorem

Statements	Reasons
1) $\angle 1$ and $\angle 7$ are supplementary.	1) Given
2) $\angle 1 \cong \angle 4$	2) Vertical Angles Theorem
3) $\angle 4$ and $\angle 7$ are supplementary.	3) _____
4) $\angle 7 \cong \angle 6$	4) _____
5) $\angle 4$ and $\angle 7$ are supplementary.	5) Substitution Property
6) $r \parallel s$	6) _____

Common Core Standards Practice   Week 5

Selected Response

1. Lines a, b, and c exist in the same coordinate plane. $a \perp b$ and $b \perp c$. Which of the following statements is true?

   A $a \parallel c$

   B $a \perp c$

   C $b \parallel c$

   D $a \parallel b$

Constructed Response

2. In $\triangle ABC$, $m\angle A = 24$, $m\angle B = x$ and $m\angle C = 2x$. Find $m\angle B$ and $m\angle C$.

Extended Response

3. Consider $\triangle ABC$. The exterior angles of $\triangle ABC$ are $\angle 1$, $\angle 2$, and $\angle 3$, respectively. Prove that the sum of the measures of the exterior angles of the triangle is 360. Use the reasons below to complete the proof. Some reasons may be used more than once.

   - Angles that form a linear pair are supplementary.
   - Triangle Angle Sum Theorem
   - Definition of supplementary angles

   - Subtraction Property of Equality
   - Addition Property of Equality
   - Substitution Property

Statements	Reasons
1) ABC is a triangle with exterior angles 1, 2, and 3.	1) Given
2) $\angle 1$ and $\angle A$ are supplementary.	2) Angles that form a linear pair are supplementary.
3) $m\angle 1 + m\angle A = 180$	3) _____
4) $\angle 2$ and $\angle B$ are supplementary.	4) Angles that form a linear pair are supplementary.
5) $m\angle 2 + m\angle B = 180$	5) _____
6) $\angle 3$ and $\angle C$ are supplementary.	6) Angles that form a linear pair are supplementary.
7) $m\angle 3 + m\angle C = 180$	7) _____
8) $m\angle 1 + m\angle A + m\angle 2 + m\angle B + m\angle 3 + m\angle C = 540$	8) _____
9) $m\angle A + m\angle B + m\angle C = 180$	9) _____
10) $m\angle 1 + m\angle 2 + m\angle 3 + 180 = 540$	10) _____
11) $m\angle 1 + m\angle 2 + m\angle 3 = 360$	11) _____

Common Core Standards Practice

Week 6

Selected Response

1. Which equation when graphed is parallel to any vertical line?

   A $x = 3$
   B $y = 4$
   C $x = y$
   D $y = x + 8$

Constructed Response

2. Construct a line through point D that is parallel to $\overline{GH}$.

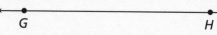

Extended Response

3. **a.** Find the slope of each line represented by an equation below.
   b. Which of the following equations represent lines that are perpendicular to the line with equation $y = 3(x - 1)$? Write each equation in the appropriate box.

   $y = 3x + 8$ $5x + 15y = 1$

   $y = -3x + 10$ $y = -\frac{1}{3}x - 5$

   $3x - 9y = 14$

Perpendicular to $y = 3(x - 1)$	Not Perpendicular to $y = 3(x - 1)$

Common Core Standards Practice   **Week 7**

Selected Response

1. If $\triangle ABC \cong \triangle DEF$, which of the following statements is true?

   A $\overline{CB} \cong \overline{FE}$
   B $\overline{AC} \cong \overline{DE}$
   C $\overline{AC} \cong \overline{EF}$
   D $\overline{BC} \cong \overline{DE}$

Constructed Response

2. Consider the points $J(2, 3)$, $K(5, 7)$, $L(8, 3)$, $M(-2, 1)$, $N(1, 5)$, $O(4, 1)$. Is $\triangle JKL \cong \triangle MNO$? Justify your answer.

Extended Response

3. **a.** Construct a triangle that is congruent to the triangle shown below. The entire triangle must be in the first quadrant, $m\angle B = 90$, and one vertex must be at $(1, 1)$.

   b. Which postulate proves that the triangles are congruent? Explain.

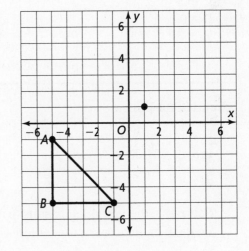

Common Core Standards Practice

Selected Response

1. △ABC is an equilateral triangle.
   △ACD ≅ △BCD; $\overline{CD}$ bisects ∠ACB.
   What is m∠DCB?

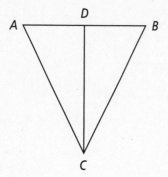

   A 15
   B 30
   C 60
   D 90

Constructed Response

2. Given:
   $AB = 12$, $BC = 2x + 3$,
   $DF = 13$, $FH = 6x - 18$
   For what value of x are the triangles congruent by the Hypotenuse-Leg Theorem?

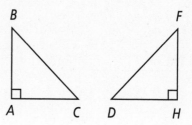

Extended Response

3. Given: △LRN is equilateral; $\overline{MR} \cong \overline{PR}$
   Prove: △MLR ≅ △PNR

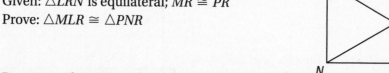

Rearrange the potential reasons to align properly with the corresponding statements. Write them in order in the middle column of the table.

Statements	Reasons	Potential Reasons
1) △LRN is equilateral; $\overline{MR} \cong \overline{PR}$	1) _____	Vertical Angles Theorem
2) $\overline{LR} \cong \overline{NR}$	2) _____	SAS Postulate
3) ∠LRM ≅ ∠NRP	3) _____	Given
4) △MLR ≅ △PNR	4) _____	Definition of equilateral △

Common Core Standards Practice   Week 9

Selected Response

1. *D* is the midpoint of $\overline{AB}$. *G* is the midpoint of $\overline{BC}$. *DG* = 5. What is *AC*?

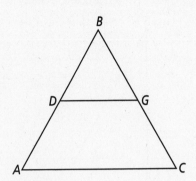

- **A** 2.5
- **B** 5
- **C** 10
- **D** 15

Constructed Response

2. What is the value of *x*?

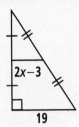

Extended Response

3. a. Prove $\overline{AB} \parallel \overline{DF}$ using the slope formula.

b. Prove $AB = \frac{1}{2}DF$ using the Distance Formula.

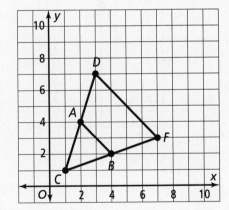

Common Core Standards Practice

Week 10

Selected Response

1. $\overline{WT}$ is the angle bisector of $\angle STR$.
If $m\angle S = m\angle R$ and $RS = 8$, what is WS?

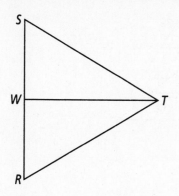

A 2
B 4
C 6
D 8

Constructed Response

2. $\overline{RS}$ is the perpendicular bisector of
$\overline{WT}$. $WS = 7x + 4$ and $ST = 53$. Find x.

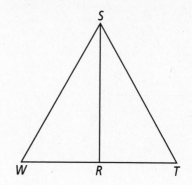

Extended Response

3. $\overline{CD}$ is the angle bisector of $\angle ACB$.
  a. Using the Distance Formula, prove that $AD = DB$.

  b. Prove that $\overline{CD}$ is the perpendicular bisector of $\overline{AB}$.

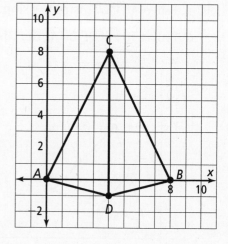

Common Core Standards Practice

Week 11

Selected Response

1. What are the coordinates of the circumcenter for $\triangle ABC$?

   $A(0, 5), B(-4, 5), C(-4, -3)$

   A $(-1, 2)$
   B $(1, -2)$
   C $(2, -1)$
   D $(-2, 1)$

Constructed Response

2. Find the value of x.

   $DE = 6x$

   $AB = 4x + 32$

   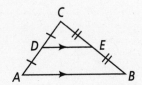

Extended Response

3. **a.** Draw an obtuse triangle and construct the inscribed and circumscribed circle.

   b. Describe your method.

Common Core Standards Practice

Week 12

Selected Response

1. What is the sum of the angle measures of a decagon?

   A 1800

   B 1440

   C 180

   D 144

Constructed Response

2. Solve to find the values of x and y in the parallelogram.

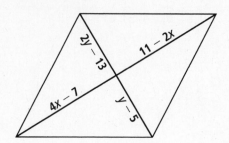

Extended Response

3. $\overline{LN}$ and $\overline{MO}$ bisect each other at P. Prove that $LMNO$ is a parallelogram.

Common Core Standards Practice

Week 13

Selected Response

1. In rectangle $ABCD$, $AC = 2x + 15$ and $DB = 5x - 12$. What is the length of a diagonal?

A 1
B 9
C 18
D 33

Constructed Response

2. Quadrilateral $WXYZ$ is an isosceles trapezoid and $m\angle Z = 74$.
What are $m\angle W$, $m\angle X$, and $m\angle Y$?

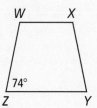

Extended Response

3. Given: $ABCD$ is a parallelogram.
$\overline{AC}$ bisects $\angle DAB$.
Prove: $\overline{AC}$ bisects $\angle DCB$.

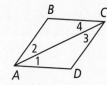

Common Core Standards Practice

Week 14

Selected Response

1. What is the most precise name for the quadrilateral defined by the following points in the coordinate plane?

   $A(1, -4), B(1, 1), C(-2, 2), D(-2, -3)$

   A kite
   B rectangle
   C isosceles trapezoid
   D parallelogram

Constructed Response

2. Quadrilateral $ABCD$ has vertices $A(0, 1), B(-1, 4), C(2, 5),$ and $D(3, 2).$

   a. Plot the points.

   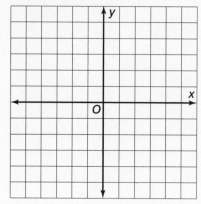

   b. Is quadrilateral $ABCD$ a rectangle? Explain.

Extended Response

3. Use the table to categorize which of the following conclusions can be reached using coordinate geometry.

   $\overline{XY} \cong \overline{ST}$ $\overline{JK}$ bisects $\overline{MN}.$ $\angle P \cong \angle O$ $\triangle ABC$ is a right triangle.
   $\overline{RS} \parallel \overline{TU}$ $\overline{WX} \perp \overline{YZ}$ $m\angle K + m\angle L = 180$

Can Be Reached	Cannot Be Reached

Common Core Standards Practice   Week 15

Selected Response

1. Are the triangles similar? If so, choose the reasoning.

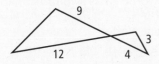

    A No, corresponding sides are not proportional.
    B Yes, Angle-Angle Similarity
    C Yes, Side-Side-Side Similarity
    D Yes, Side-Angle-Side Similarity

Constructed Response

2. **a.** Explain why the triangles are similar.
    b. Solve for the value of x.

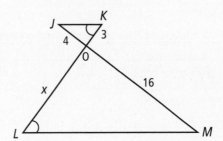

Extended Response

3. Quadrilateral $ABCD$ has vertices $A(1, 1)$, $B(5, 3)$, $C(3, -1)$, and $D(-1, -3)$.
    a. Plot the points and draw diagonals.
    b. What is the best classification for the quadrilateral? Explain your reasoning.

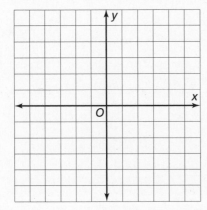

Common Core Standards Practice   **Week 16**

Selected Response

1. Which of the following reason(s) help(s) prove $\frac{ME}{ED} = \frac{NF}{FD}$?

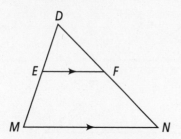

  A Angle-Angle Similarity
  B Side-Angle-Side Theorem
  C Side-Splitter Theorem
  D Pythagorean Theorem

Constructed Response

2. A yardstick that is perpendicular to the ground casts a 5-ft shadow. At the same time, a utility pole casts a shadow that is 6 yd long.

  a. Draw a diagram of this scenario.

  b. How tall is the utility pole?

Extended Response

3. Prove $\frac{VS}{VT} = \frac{WU}{WT}$.

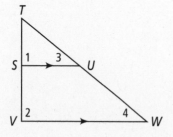

Common Core Standards Practice

Week 17

Selected Response

1. What is the value of x?

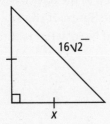

   A 8

   B $8\sqrt{2}$

   C 16

   D $16\sqrt{2}$

Constructed Response

2. Find the values of w and x to the nearest degree.

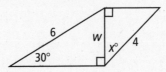

Extended Response

3. To hang a 9-ft hammock from a tree, you first tie one end to the trunk of the tree. When the hammock is tied on one end, it makes a 20° angle with the ground.

   a. Use a compass and protractor to model this scenario.

   b. How far up the tree is the hammock tied on? Round your answer to the nearest foot.

Common Core Standards Practice

Week 18

Selected Response

1. In $\triangle ABC$, $AB = 24$, $BC = 36$, and $m\angle A = 118$. What is $m\angle C$?

   A about 1
   B about 21
   C about 36
   D about 54

Constructed Response

2. A center fielder catches a fly ball in the outfield. Her distance to the shortstop is 80 ft, as shown in the figure. If she is 135 ft away from first base, what is the value of x?

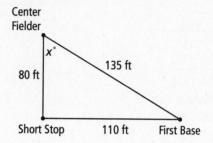

Extended Response

3. A cruise ship has sailed 1130 mi from the port in Alaska. From the ship, the captain records an angle measurement between the port in Alaska and the port in Canada as 53°. He knows the angle from the port in Alaska between the ship and the port in Canada is 88°.

   a. Draw a diagram of the ship's position.

   b. To the nearest mile, how far is the ship from the port in Canada? Explain how you know

Common Core Standards Practice

Week 19

Selected Response

1. Find the coordinates of the image.

   $R_{x\text{-axis}} (7, -2)$

   A $(-2, 7)$
   B $(-7, -2)$
   C $(-7, 2)$
   D $(7, 2)$

Constructed Response

2. **a.** What are the vertices of
   $T_{<-3, -5>} (ABCD)$?
   b. Graph the image of $ABCD$.

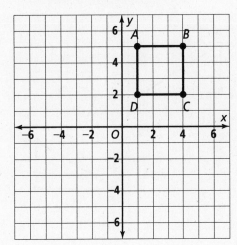

Extended Response

3. **a.** Plot the points $A(-3, 2)$, $B(-1, 3)$, $C(-1, 1)$.

   b. Graph the image of $\triangle ABC$ after the given transformation.
   $(R_{x\text{-axis}} \circ r_{(180°, o)})(\triangle ABC)$

   c. Describe another transformation that will make the same image.

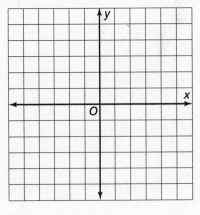

Common Core Standards Practice

Selected Response

1. In the diagram below, $\triangle ABC \cong \triangle XYZ$. What is a congruence transformation that maps $\triangle ABC$ onto $\triangle XYZ$?

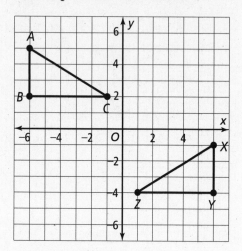

  A $R_{y\text{-axis}} \circ T_{<-6,\,0>}$
  B $R_{x\text{-axis}} \circ T_{<6,\,0>}$
  C $r_{(180°,\,O)} \circ T_{<0,\,-1>}$
  D $R_{x\text{-axis}} \circ r_{(180°,\,O)}$

Constructed Response

2. The figure below shows two congruent rectangles. What are four different isometries that map the top rectangle onto the bottom rectangle?

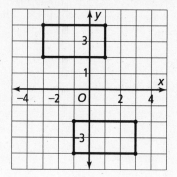

Extended Response

3. Verify the ASA postulate for triangle congruence by using congruence transformations.

  Given: $\overline{AB} \cong \overline{XY}$, $\angle A \cong \angle X$, $\angle B \cong \angle Y$

  Prove: $\triangle XYZ \cong \triangle ABC$

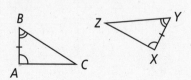

Common Core Standards Practice

Selected Response

1. Is $D_{(n, A)}(\triangle ABC) = \triangle A'B'C'$ an enlargement or a reduction? What is the scale factor n of the dilation?

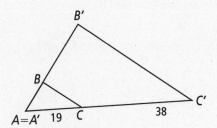

A enlargement; $n = 3$
B enlargement; $n = \frac{1}{3}$
C reduction; $n = 3$
D reduction; $n = \frac{1}{3}$

Constructed Response

2. $ABCD$ has vertices $A(1, 3)$, $B(-2, 3)$, $C(-4, -3)$, $D(-1, -3)$.
   a. Graph $ABCD$.
   b. Graph $A'B'C'D'$, the image of $ABCD$ after a dilation with center $(0, 0)$ and a scale factor of 3.

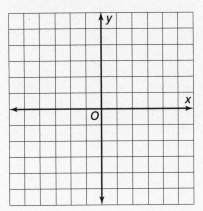

Extended Response

3. An army captain wants to use similar triangles to determine the distance d across the drop zone shown below.

   a. Are the two triangles similar? Explain your reasoning.

   b. What is the distance across the drop zone?

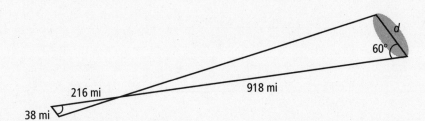

Common Core Standards Practice

Week 22

Selected Response

1. Find the area of the triangle to the nearest square inch.

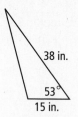

38 in.

53°

15 in.

  A 171 in.^{2}
  B 228 in.^{2}
  C 455 in.^{2}
  D 910 in.^{2}

Constructed Response

2. Two similar trapezoids have areas 98 in.^{2} and 242 in.^{2}.

   a. What is the scale factor?

   b. What is the ratio of their perimeters?

Extended Response

3. a. Describe two different methods for finding the area of the floor of a stage that is shaped like the regular hexagon ABCDEF.

   b. What is the area?

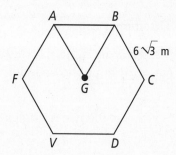

Common Core Standards Practice   **Week 23**

Selected Response

1. What is the area of sector *ABC*?

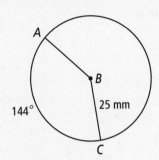

A 625π mm^2
B 625 mm^2
C 250π mm^2
D 250 mm^2

Constructed Response

2. Find the length of minor arc *AB*.

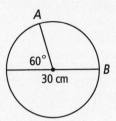

Extended Response

3. Circles *A* and *B* each have a radius of 10 and *AB* = 10.
   a. Draw a diagram that shows both circles.

   b. Find the area of the region that is contained by both circles.

Common Core Standards Practice

Week 24

Selected Response

1. What shape is formed by the cross section of a triangular pyramid with a horizontal plane?

   A pentagon
   B rectangle
   C square
   D triangle

Constructed Response

2. a. Sketch a polyhedron with faces that are all rectangles.

   b. Draw two different nets for the polyhedron.

Extended Response

3. Draw the net of each regular polyhedron.

a.

b.

c.

Common Core Standards Practice

Week 25

Selected Response

1. What is the volume of a cylinder with a diameter of 4 in. and a height of 10 in.? Round your answer to the nearest cubic inch.

   A 40 in.^3

   B 126 in.^3

   C 160 in.^3

   D 400 in.^3

Constructed Response

2. A conference center is in the shape of a square pyramid with a base length of 219.8 m and a height of 174.34 m. To the nearest cubic meter, what is the approximate volume of the conference center?

Extended Response

3. A vendor presses a full scoop of frozen yogurt into a cone. The frozen yogurt has a diameter of 7 cm. The cone has a height of 14 cm and a base diameter the width of the frozen yogurt. If the frozen yogurt melts into the cone, will the cone overflow? Explain.

Common Core Standards Practice

Week 26

Selected Response

1. A pyramid has a volume of 108 m^3. A similar pyramid has base edges and a height that are $\frac{1}{3}$ of the length of those in the original pyramid. What is the volume of the smaller pyramid?

   A 36 m^3
   B 24 m^3
   C 12 m^3
   D 4 m^3

Constructed Response

2. A spherical balloon can hold a volume of 2 cm^3 of helium. If the radius of the balloon is quadrupled, how much helium can the new balloon hold?

Extended Response

3. List these solids in order from the one with the least volume to the one with the greatest volume.

   A a cube with edge 5 cm
   B a cylinder with radius 4 cm and height 4 cm
   C a square pyramid with base edges 6 cm and height 6 cm
   D a cone with radius 4 cm and height 9 cm
   E a rectangular prism with base 5 cm-by-5 cm and height 6 cm

Common Core Standards Practice   Week 27

Selected Response

1. What is the value of *x* to the nearest tenth?

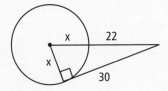

A 4.8 units

B 9.5 units

C 31.5 units

D 372 units

Constructed Response

2. Use the arc below to find the center of the circle that contains the arc. Explain the process.

Extended Response

3. Classify each angle/arc measure as greater than 90, less than 90, or equal to 90.

Greater than 90	Less than 90	Equal to 90

Common Core Standards Practice

Week 28

Selected Response

1. Which of the following describe the circle represented by the following equation.

$$(x + 17)^2 + (y - 14)^2 = 196$$

   A center $(-17, 14)$
   B center $(17, 14)$
   C center $(-17, -14)$
   D center $(17, -14)$
   E radius 14
   F radius 196

Constructed Response

2. Write an equation for the locus of points in the coordinate plane that are 11 units from $(0, -8)$.

Extended Response

3. The diameter of Mars is about 6792 km.

   a. Write an equation that represents the equator on the surface of Mars with the center of Mars as the origin.

   b. Find the length of a 1-degree arc on the equator of Mars to the nearest tenth of a kilometer.

   c. If it takes a Mars rover 1 hr to navigate 3 km on the surface of Mars, estimate how long it will take the rover to circumnavigate Mars.

Common Core Standards Practice   Week 29

Selected Response

1. You are playing a board game with two standard number cubes. It is your last turn and if you roll a number greater than 4, you will win the game. What is the probability that you will NOT win the game?

   A $\frac{2}{3}$

   B $\frac{1}{3}$

   C $\frac{1}{4}$

   D $\frac{1}{6}$

Constructed Response

2. The results from a survey of 150 students from Central High are shown below.

   a. Make a probability distribution table of the number of children in the families of Central High students.

   b. If Central High has 953 students, predict the number of families that will have exactly 3 children.

   c. How many families will have either two or three children?

Number of Children in Family	Frequency
1	38
2	42
3	30
4	27
More than 4	13

Extended Response

3. A member of a band told the band that there are 3,991,680 different ways to choose 7 out of 12 songs that the band wants to play at the upcoming show. Explain the error in his statement and find the correct answer.

Common Core Standards Practice

Week 30

Selected Response

1. A particular basketball team has a 75% chance of winning a tournament if its star player is able to play. Otherwise, the team has a 40% chance of winning. The doctor says that the star player has a 60% chance of being able to play. What is the probability that the team will win the tournament?

   A 67%
   B 61%
   C 55%
   D 48%

Constructed Response

2. In a survey of shoppers, 54% use coupons, 36% belong to shoppers clubs, and 18% use coupons and belong to shoppers clubs.

   a. What is the conditional probability that a shopper uses coupons given that he or she belongs to shoppers clubs?

   b. What is the conditional probability that a shopper belongs to shoppers clubs given that he or she uses coupons?

Extended Response

3. A soccer team wins 65% of its games on muddy fields and 30% of its games on dry fields. The probability of the field being muddy for its next game is 70%.

   a. What is the probability that the team will win its next game?

   b. If the probability of the field being muddy decreases, how will that influence the probability of the team winning its next game?

End-of-Course Assessment

Selected Response

Read each question. Then circle the letter(s) of the correct answer(s). There may be more than one correct response.

1. What value of x makes $\triangle FGH$ similar to $\triangle MNP$?

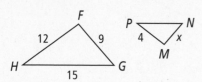

A 3

B 3.75

C 5.3

D 27

2. Write an equation of a circle with center $(-1, 2)$ passing through the point $(2, 4)$.

A $(x + 1)^2 + (y - 2)^2 = 13$

B $(x - 1)^2 + (y + 2)^2 = 13$

C $(x + 1)^2 + (y - 2)^2 = 169$

D $(x - 1)^2 + (y + 2)^2 = 169$

3. Which equation(s) can be used to find the value of x?

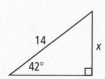

A $\cos 48° = \frac{x}{14}$

B $\sin 42° = \frac{x}{14}$

C $\cos 42° = \frac{14}{x}$

D $\sin 48° = \frac{x}{14}$

4. Find the volume of a cone with diameter 16 cm and height 12 cm.

A 100.5 cm³

B 804.2 cm³

C 2412.7 cm³

D 3217.0 cm³

5. A railway club provides free train rides on their large circular tracks. There are two tracks. The distance from Track 1 to the center is 30 m. The distance between Track 1 and Track 2 is 5 m. How much farther is the train ride on Track 2 than Track 1?

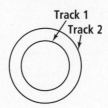

A 15.7 m

B 31.4 m

C 78.5 m

D 157.1 m

6. Which theorem(s) can you use to prove that the two triangles are congruent?

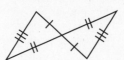

A ASA

B AAS

C SSS

D SAS

7. Choose all the ways you can correctly name plane *P*.

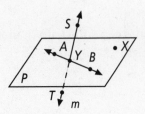

A plane *AYB*

B plane *AYX*

C plane *YBP*

D plane *YBX*

8. Choose all angle pairs that are congruent.

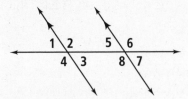

A ∠1 and ∠5

B ∠1 and ∠6

C ∠2 and ∠8

D ∠4 and ∠6

9. A dilation maps points *B*, *C*, and *D* onto *B′*, *C′*, and *D′* respectively. Choose all of the true statements.

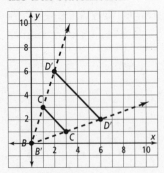

A $\overline{CD} \parallel \overline{C'D'}$

B The scale factor is $\frac{1}{2}$.

C $\dfrac{BC}{B'C'} = \dfrac{BD}{B'D'}$

D △*BCD* ≅ △*B′C′D′*

10. Which equation(s) represent a line that contains the point (−8, 3) and is perpendicular to $y = 4x - 7$?

A $x + 4y = 4$

B $y = 4x - 20$

C $y = -\frac{1}{4}x + 1$

D $y = -\frac{1}{4}x + 35$

11. Which statement(s) are true?

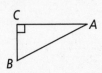

A $\cos A = \sin B$

B $\sin A = \cos A$

C $\sin A = \cos B$

D $\tan A = \tan B$

12. Which edges of the prism are parallel to $\overline{AD}$?

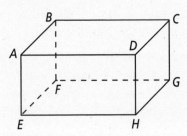

A $\overline{BC}$

B $\overline{EF}$

C $\overline{FG}$

D $\overline{DH}$

13. The map below shows a section of a city. Which statement(s) are true?

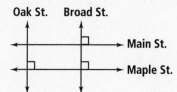

Oak St.   Broad St.

Main St.

Maple St.

    A Oak Street is perpendicular to Main Street.
    B Broad Street is parallel to Oak Street.
    C Main Street is parallel to Maple Street.
    D Oak Street is perpendicular to Broad Street.

14. Which shape is formed by a vertical plane intersecting the cone below? [G.GMD.4, Lesson 11-1]

    A circle
    B trapezoid
    C triangle
    D parallelogram

15. A bar of silver is shaped like a trapezoidal prism. The dimensions of the base are shown below. If the height of the bar is 12 cm, what is its volume to the nearest tenth?

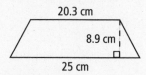

20.3 cm

8.9 cm

25 cm

    A 325.3 cm^3
    B 2419 cm^3
    C 2670 cm^3
    D 3261.6 cm^3

16. Find the area of the sector.

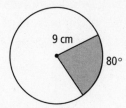

9 cm

80°

    A 4π cm^2
    B 9π cm^2
    C 12π cm^2
    D 18π cm^2

17. What are all of the correct ways to describe why the triangles below are congruent?

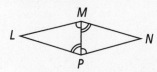

M

L

N

P

    A ASA Congruence Theorem
    B A reflection of $\triangle MNP$ across $\overline{MP}$ is a rigid motion that maps $\triangle MNP$ onto $\triangle PLM$.
    C A translation, followed by a reflection, and then another translation is a series of rigid motions that will map $\triangle MNP$ onto $\triangle PLM$.
    D A rotation of $\triangle MLP$ about point M, followed by a translation is a series of rigid motions that maps $\triangle MLP$ onto $\triangle PNM$.

18. What are all the possible coordinates for point M such that $SM = \frac{1}{2}MT$?

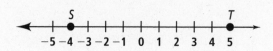

S T

−5 −4 −3 −2 −1   0   1   2   3   4   5

    A −13
    B −2
    C −1
    D 13

19. A lifeguard sits on the shore in a chair that is 6 ft above the ground. She sees a swimmer at an angle of depression of 10°. About how far away from shore is the swimmer?

A 6.1 ft

B 34.0 ft

C 34.6 ft

D 95.1 ft

20. Which of the following statements is sufficient to show that a similarity transformation exists that maps △PQR to△P′Q′R′?

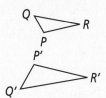

A $\angle P \cong \angle P'$ and $\angle Q \cong \angle Q'$

B $\overline{PR} \cong \overline{P'R'}$

C $\dfrac{PQ}{QR} = \dfrac{P'Q'}{Q'R'}$

D $QP = Q'P'$ and $QR = Q'R'$

21. Triangle *ABC* is reflected across line *m*. Which statement(s) are true?

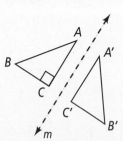

A $\overline{A'C'}$ is perpendicular to $\overline{C'B'}$.

B $AB = A'B'$

C $m\angle A = m\angle A'$

D $CC' = BB'$

22. *LMNK* is a parallelogram. What are the values of *x* and *y*?

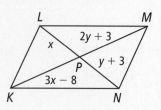

A $x = 4, y = 4$

B $x = 5, y = 2$

C $x = 9, y = 3$

D $x = 8, y = 11$

23. If an angle of one triangle is congruent to an angle of a second triangle, and the sides that include the two angles are proportional, then what is true about the two triangles?

A The triangles are similar.

B The triangles are congruent.

C The triangles are neither similar nor congruent.

D There is not enough information to make a determination.

24. Find the value of *x* to the nearest tenth.

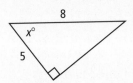

A 32.0   **C** 51.3

B 38.7   **D** 58

25. What is the length of $\overline{PQ}$?

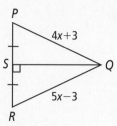

A 24   **C** 30

B 27   **D** 32

Constructed Response

In this section, show all your work in the space beneath each test item.

26. Write an equation of a line parallel to $y = \frac{1}{2}x + 3$ that passes through $(2, 5)$.

27. If $\sin F = \frac{3}{5}$, what is $\cos G$?

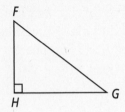

28. An environmental group is making signs for an upcoming community recycling day. They want the signs to be equilateral triangles with heights of 35 in. How long in inches will each side of the signs be? Round your answer to the nearest tenth of an inch.

29. Is $D_{(n, X)}(\triangle XYZ) = \triangle X'Y'Z'$ an enlargement or a reduction? What is the scale factor n of the dilation?

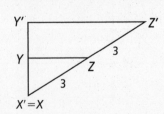

30. What are the vertices of $T_{<3, -1>}(\triangle FGH)$? Graph the image of $\triangle FGH$.

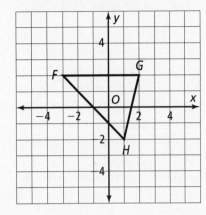

31. Construct $\overleftrightarrow{AB}$ that is perpendicular to line m.

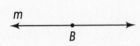

32. Constructs $\angle S$ congruent to $\angle R$.

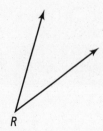

33. Determine whether the parallelograms are similar. If so, write a similarity statement and give the scale factor. If they are not similar, explain why.

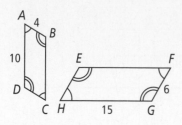

34. Which can has a greater volume? How much greater? Round your answer to the nearest cubic inch.

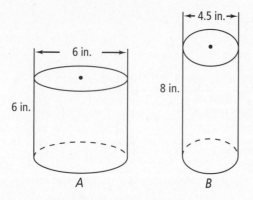

35. The measure of ∠5 is 110. Write each angle in the correct column.

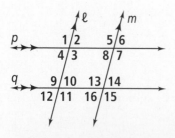

Angles that are congruent to ∠5	Angles that are congruent to ∠8

36. Does the transformation appear to be a rigid motion? Explain.

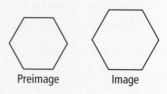

37. The diagonals of a quadrilateral are congruent and perpendicular. Identify the quadrilateral.

38. A student says that if two sides and one angle of one triangle are congruent to any two sides and one angle of another triangle, then the two triangles are congruent. What mistake did the student make? Draw two triangles that show the student is incorrect.

39. Draw and label the reflection of square *LMNP* across line *t*. Then describe how you know that *LMNP* and its image are congruent in terms of rigid motions.

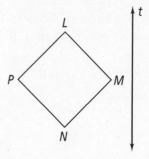

40. The coordinates of the vertices of $\triangle ABC$ are $A(0, 0)$, $B(6, 2)$ and $C(2, -4)$. What are the coordinates of the vertices after a dilation of $\frac{1}{2}$, followed by a reflection across the y-axis?

41. Draw the lines of symmetry and give the angle(s) of rotation for the figure below.

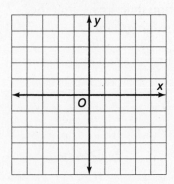

42. Describe the shape of the vertical and horizontal cross-sections of the cylinder below.

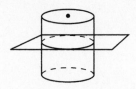

43. Determine if there is a similarity transformation that maps one figure onto another. If so, describe the transformation and write a similarity statement. If not, explain why.

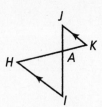

44. Rectangle $ABCD$ has vertices $A(3, 5)$, $B(5, 5)$, $C(5, 1)$, and $D(3, 1)$. What are the coordinates of the vertices of $r_{(90°,\ O)}(ABCD)$?

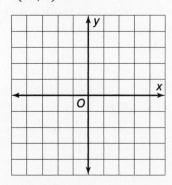

45. Find the perimeter of $\triangle TAP$ with vertices $T(1, 4)$, $A(4, 4)$, and $P(3, 0)$ to the nearest tenth.

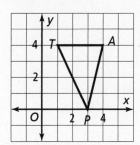

46. Show that the circles are similar by finding a scale factor and describing a similarity transformation that maps circle P to circle Q.

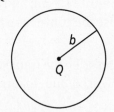

47. How can you use a congruence transformation to show that the figures are congruent?

48. Annie will use two right triangles to make a square for a logo. The triangles have the same side lengths and angle measures. What must also be true about the triangles in order to guarantee that the opposite sides of the square are parallel? Explain.

49. Find a congruence transformation that maps $\triangle CDF$ to $\triangle HJK$.

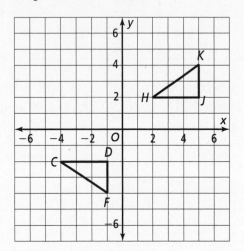

50. You can find the density of an object by using $d = \frac{m}{V}$, where m is the mass of the object in grams and V is the volume in milliliters. What is the density of a can of tomato sauce with diameter 10 cm, height 11.5 cm, and a mass of 822 grams? Use the conversion factor 1 cm^3 = 1 mL.

51. Describe the transformations that map Figure 1 onto Figure 3.

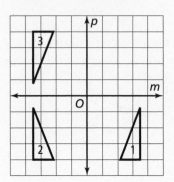

52. Construct an equilateral triangle. Label any congruent sides or angles.

53. The three sides of $\triangle RST$ are congruent to the three sides of $\triangle XYZ$. Describe a rigid motion that proves that the triangles are congruent.

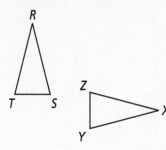

54. A diagram of a water tower is shown below. How can you use a geometric model to find the volume of the water tank at the top of the tower? Find the approximate volume. Use 3.14 for π.

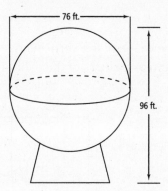

55. Write a congruence statement relating triangles in the figure below.

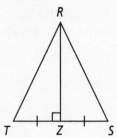

Extended Response

In this section, show all your work in the space beneath each test item.

56. Write a two-column proof to prove the Vertical Angles Theorem.

    Given: $\angle 1$ and $\angle 3$ are vertical angles.

    Prove: $\angle 1 \cong \angle 3$

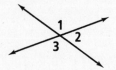

57. Write a proof to show that the diagonals of a rectangle are congruent.

    Given: Rectangle $ABCD$

    Prove: $\overline{AC} \cong \overline{BD}$

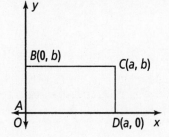

58. Given: $\overleftrightarrow{DL} \perp \overline{GP}$, $\overleftrightarrow{DL}$ bisects $\overline{GP}$

Prove: $GD = PD$

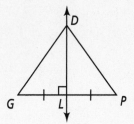

59. Prove that the diagonals of a parallelogram bisect each other.

Given: $\square ABCD$

Prove: $\overline{AC}$ and $\overline{BD}$ bisect each other at point E.

60. The state of Colorado is shaped like a rectangle with an approximate width of 280 mi and length of 380 mi. What is the population density of Colorado in people per square mile if the population is 5,116,800?

61. The figure shows a pyramid inscribed in a cube. The volume of the pyramid is 72 cm^3. Use the diagram and explain the relationship between the volume of the cube and the volume of the pyramid.

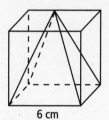

6 cm

62. Quadrilateral $ABDC$ is inscribed in a circle. Prove that $m\angle A + m\angle D = 180$.

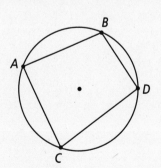

63. Write a two-column proof.

Given: $\triangle XYZ$ with $\overleftrightarrow{PQ} \parallel \overleftrightarrow{XZ}$

Prove: $\dfrac{XP}{PY} = \dfrac{ZQ}{QY}$

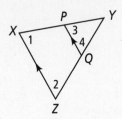

64. Prove the Triangle Angle-Sum Theorem.

Given: $\triangle GHK$

Prove: $m\angle G + m\angle H + m\angle K = 180$

65. *GMPA* and *GRJF* are parallelograms. GRA is an equilateral triangle. Prove that $m\angle F = m\angle P$.

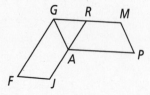

Performance Task: Designing a Container

Complete this performance task in the space provided. Fully answer all parts of the performance task with detailed responses. You should provide sound mathematical reasoning to support your work.

Three teams of students are designing containers that will hold 1000 mL of liquid. The containers must be 10 cm high and be open at the top. The shapes that the teams plan to use for their containers are listed below.

Team 1: rectangular prism with a square base

Team 2: cylinder

Team 3: cone

Task Description

Which team needs the least amount of material to make its container? Which team needs the most material? (Recall that 1 mL = 1 cm^3. Round your answers to the nearest hundredth.)

a. What are the dimensions of Team 1's container? Considering the outside of the container only, what is the surface area?

b. What are the dimensions and surface area of Team 2's container?

Performance Task: Designing a Container (continued)

c. What are the dimensions and surface area of Team 3's container?

d. Which team needs the least amount of material to make its container? Which team needs the most?

e. Suppose Team 2's cylindrical container does NOT have to be 10 cm high. Can you change the container's dimensions to use less material but still hold 1000 mL of liquid? Show your work.

Performance Task: Urban Planning

Complete this performance task in the space provided. Fully answer all parts of the performance task with detailed responses. You should provide sound mathematical reasoning to support your work.

Students are designing a new town as part of a social studies project on urban planning. They want to place the town's high school at point *A* and the middle school at point *B*. They also plan to build roads that run directly from point *A* to the mall and from point *B* to the mall. The average cost to build a road in this area is $550,000 per mile.

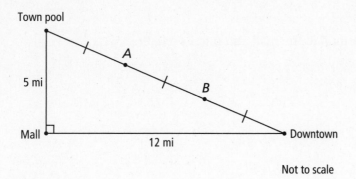

Not to scale

Task Description

What is the difference in the cost of the roads built to the Mall from the two schools?

a. Find the measure of each acute angle of the right triangle shown.

b. Find the length of the hypotenuse. Also find the length of each of the three congruent segments forming the hypotenuse.

Performance Task: Urban Planning (continued)

c. Draw the road from point *A* to the mall and find its length.

d. Draw the road from point *B* to the mall and find its length.

e. How much farther from the mall is point *B* than point *A*? How much more will it cost to build the longer road?

Performance Task: Analyzing an Excavation Site

Complete this performance task in the space provided. Fully answer all parts of the performance task with detailed responses. You should provide sound mathematical reasoning to support your work.

Archeologists find evidence of three houses at a dig site. They believe the houses were arranged in a circle and want to excavate at the center of the settlement. The map shows the locations of the three houses, at points *A*, *B*, and *C*.

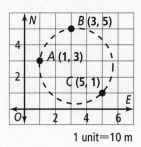

1 unit=10 m

Task Description

Find the coordinates of the center of the settlement, and how far each house was from the center.

a. For any chord of a circle, the perpendicular bisector of the chord passes through the circle's center. Explain how you can use this fact to find the center of the circle.

Performance Task: Analyzing an Excavation Site (continued)

b. Find the midpoints of $\overline{AB}$ and $\overline{BC}$.

c. Find the slopes of $\overline{AB}$ and $\overline{BC}$.

d. Use the midpoints and slopes of $\overline{AB}$ and $\overline{BC}$ to write equations for the perpendicular bisectors of these segments.

e. What are the coordinates of the settlement's center? Explain.

f. How far was each house from the center of the settlement?

g. Give possible coordinates of another house in the settlement.

Performance Task: Applying Geometric Probability

Complete this performance task in the space provided. Fully answer all parts of the performance task with detailed responses. You should provide sound mathematical reasoning to support your work.

Students are competing in a class event, throwing darts at a square dartboard like the one shown below. The points for hitting each region are as shown. All triangles on the dartboard are equilateral triangles, and triangles with the same number of points are the same size.

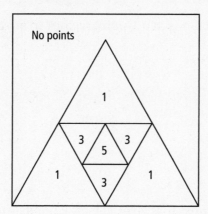

Task Description

You and your friend are playing a game of darts. You have 43 points and your friend has 48 points, but you have 2 darts left to throw and your friend has none. If each dart lands in a random location on the board, what is the probability that you can take the lead and win the game with your last 2 darts?

a. What is the probability that a dart hitting the board lands anywhere within the largest triangle?

Performance Task: Applying Geometric Probability (continued)

b. What is the probability that a dart hitting the board does NOT land in any triangle?

c. What is the probability that a dart lands in a 1-point region? In a 3-point region? In the 5-point region?

d. List each sequence of two dart throws that gives at least 6 points, and therefore wins the game. What is the probability of getting each winning sequence?

e. What is the probability that you get *any* of the sequences from part (d) and win the game?